365
Reflections on
MOTHERS

365

Reflections on

MOTHERS

Selected and arranged by
Dahlia Porter and Gabriel Cervantes

Adams Media Corporation
Holbrook, Massachusetts

Published by Adams Media Corporation
260 Center Street, Holbrook, MA 02343

ISBN: 1-58062-008-6

Printed in Canada.

J I H G F E D C

Library of Congress Cataloging-in-Publication Data
365 reflections on mothers / selected and arranged
by Dahlia Porter and Gabriel Cervantes.
p.   cm.
ISBN 1-58062-008-6 (paperback)
1. Mothers–Quotations. I. Porter, Dahlia. II. Cervantes, Gabriel.
PN6084.M6A134   1998
306.874'3–dc21   97-47045
CIP

Photo by ©TSM/Ronnie Kaufman

This book is available at quantity discounts for bulk purchases.
For information, call 1-800-872-5627 (in Massachusetts, 781-767-8100).

Visit our home page at http://www.adamsmedia.com

For Helen and Rosemary
who made us all that we are

Contents

❧

My Mother

$\mathcal{M}$y mother was the most beautiful woman I ever saw. . . . All I am I owe to my mother.

—*George Washington*

$\mathcal{M}$om, I love you and I thank you for what you did for me, but I'll never tell you, so I'll have to put it in a song.

—*Garth Brooks*

$\mathscr{M}$y mother was the source from
which I derived the guiding
principles of my life.

—*John Wesley*

$\mathcal{I}$f the whole world were put into one scale, and my mother in the other, the world would kick the beam.

—*Lord Langdale*

$\mathcal{M}$y mother gave me the example of the completely dedicated life. In my father this was translated into action, and in my mother into silence. We all live from what woman has taught us of the sublime.

—*Pope Paul II*

I had the most satisfactory of childhoods because Mother, small, delicate-boned, witty, and articulate, turned out to be exactly my age.

—*Kay Boyle*

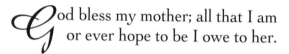

*G*od bless my mother; all that I am
or ever hope to be I owe to her.

—*Abraham Lincoln*

*W*hatever beauty or poetry is to be
found in my little book is owing
to your interest in and encouragement of
all my efforts from the first to the last;
and if ever I do anything to be proud of,
my greatest happiness will be that I can
thank you for that, as I may do for all
the good there is in me; and I shall be
content to write if it gives you pleasure.

—*Louisa May Alcott,*
in a letter to her mother

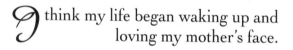 think my life began waking up and
loving my mother's face.

— *George Eliot*

$\mathcal{I}$ am aglow with the rapture of the revelation that she is the most beautiful thing in the whole world, my mother.

—Adele Wiseman

$\mathcal{Y}$ou are like an everlasting
friendship.
Your are like a secret
almost too wonderful to keep.
You are like the beginning, end and
everything in between.
You are like a spring shower.
You are like the sun shining on me and
keeping me warm.

You are like a wild flower in the
meadow.
You are like a very knowledgeable
volume of encyclopedias.
You are like you and I love you.

—*Laurel O. Hoye, aged eight,*
of her mother

$\mathcal{M}$y mother loved children—she would have given anything if I had been one.

—*Groucho Marx*

$\mathcal{M}$y mother was a wit, but never a sentimental one. Once, when somebody in our house stepped on our cat's paw, she turned to the cat and said sternly, "I *told* you not to go around barefoot!"

—*Zero Mostel*

By no amount of agile exercising of a wistful imagination could my mother have been called lenient. Generous she was: indulgent, never. Kind, yes; permissive never. In her world, people she accepted paddled their own canoes, pulled their own weight, put their own shoulders to their own plows and pushed like hell.

—*Maya Angelou*

$\mathcal{I}$ . . . have a cup of coffee with my mother. We get along very well, veterans of a guerilla war we never understood.

—*Joan Didion*

$\mathcal{M}$y own momma done better than she could and my momma's momma, *she* done better than I could. And *everybody's momma* done better than any right to expect she would. And that's the truth.

—*June Jordan*

$\mathcal{I}$ had grown big, but my mother
was bigger, and that would
always be so.

—*Jamaica Kincaid*

*C*ven if I say my mother was mean,
    I still love her and anyhow she
    wasn't *that* mean. I exaggerate
        everything I fear.

                    —*Anne Sexton,*
                    to her daughter

$\mathcal{Y}$es, Mother . . . I can see you are flawed. You have not hidden it. That is your greatest gift to me.

—*Alice Walker*

$\mathcal{P}$erhaps you still don't realize . . .
how very much I have admired
you: for your work, your teaching, your
strength and your creation of our
exquisite home . . . I don't think I've
ever specifically told you all that I love
and revere, and it is a great, great deal!

—*Sylvia Plath,*
to her mother

$\mathcal{M}$y mother had great deal of
trouble with me but I
think she enjoyed it.

—*Mark Twain*

$\mathcal{M}$y mother phones daily to ask, "Did you just try to reach me?" When I reply, "No," she adds, "So if you're not too busy, call me while I'm still alive," and hangs up.

— *Erma Bombeck*

$\mathcal{O}$ne day mother called me . . . and she said, "Forty-nine million Americans saw you on television tonight. One of them is the father of my future grandchild, but he's never going to call you because you wore your glasses."

—*Lesley Stahl*

$\mathcal{W}$hatever success comes to me
seems incomplete because
you are so often not at my side
to be glad with me.

—*Helen Keller,*
to her mother

In all my efforts to read, my mother shared fully my ambition and sympathized with me in every way she could. If I have done anything in life worth attention, I feel sure I inherited the disposition from my mother.

—*Booker T. Washington*

$\mathcal{N}$ow that I am in my forties, she tells me I'm beautiful; now that I am in my forties she sends me presents and we have the long, personal and even remarkably honest phone calls I always wanted so intensely I forbade myself to imagine them. How strange. Perhaps Shaw was correct and if we lived to be several hundred years old, we would finally work it all out. I am deeply grateful. With my poems, I finally won even my mother. The longest wooing in my life.

—*Marge Piercy*

$\mathcal{M}$y mother was my first
jealous lover.

—*Barbara Grizzuti Harrison*

$\mathcal{I}$ am all the time talking about you, and bragging, to one person or another. I am like the Ancient Mariner, who had a tale in his heart he must unfold to all. I am always button-holing somebody and saying, "Someday you must meet my mother." And then

I am off. And nothing stops me till the waiters close up the café. I do love you so much, my mother. . . . If I didn't keep calling you mother, anybody reading this would think I was writing to my sweetheart. And he would be quite right.

—*Edna St. Vincent Millay*

*N*o doubt each one of your children thinks that he or she loves you most, and so do I. . . . For me you are the most beautiful and wonderful person in the whole world; merely the fact that you are alive makes the whole world different.

—*Karen Blixen (Isak Dinesen),*
in a letter to her mother

$\mathscr{A}$t that moment, I missed my mother more than I had ever imagined possible and only wanted to live somewhere quiet and beautiful with her alone, but also at that moment I only wanted to see her lying dead, and in a coffin at my feet.

—*Jamaica Kincaid*

[My mother] said that if I listened
to her, later I would know
what she knew; where true words came
from, always from up high, above
everything else. And if I didn't listen to
her, she said my ear would bend too
easily to other people, all saying words
that had no lasting meaning, because
they came from the bottom of their
hearts, where their own desires lived, a
place where I could not belong.

—*Amy Tan*

$\mathcal{T}$hat lovely voice; how I should
weep for joy if I could
hear it now!

—*Colette, in* My Mother's House

$\mathcal{M}$y Mother! when I learn'd that
thou wast dead,
Say, wast thou conscious
of the tears I shed?
Hover'd thy spirit o'er thy sorrowing son,
Wretch even then, life's journey
just begun?

Perhaps thou gav'st me, though unseen,
a kiss;
Perhaps a tear, if souls can weep
in bliss—
Ah, that maternal smile! it answers—Yes.

—*William Cowper*

$\mathcal{M}$y mother is everywhere . . .
In the perfume of a rose,
The eyes of a tiger,
The pages of a book,
The food that we partake,
The whistling wind of the desert,
The blazing gems of sunset,
The crystal light of full moon,
The opal veils of sunshine.

—*Grace Seton-Thompson*

Her
Strength

These remarkable women of olden times are like ancient painted glass—the art of making them is lost; my mother was less than her mother, and I am less than my mother.

—*Harriet Beecher Stowe*

$\mathcal{M}$y mother wasn't what the world would call a good woman. She never said she was. And many people, including the police, said she was a bad woman. But she never agreed with them, and she had a way of lifting up her head when she talked back to them that made me know she was right.

—*Boxcar Bertha*

$\mathcal{W}$henever I feel myself inferior to everything about me, threatened by my own mediocrity, frightened by the discovery that a muscle is losing its strength, a desire its power, or a pain the keen edge of its bite, I can still hold up my head and say to myself: . . . "Let me not forget that

I am the daughter of a woman who bent her head, trembling, between the blades of a cactus, her wrinkled face full of ecstasy over the promise of a flower, a woman who herself never ceased to flower, untiringly, during three quarters of a century."

—*Colette*

$\mathcal{M}$y mother is a woman who speaks
with her life as much as
with her tongue.

—*Kesaya E. Noda*

$\mathcal{O}$n the dark womb where I began
My mother's life made me
a man.
Through all the months of human birth
Her beauty fed my common earth.

—*John Masefield*

$\mathcal{S}$ure I love the dear silver that shines
in your hair,
And the brow that's all furrowed, and
wrinkled with care.
I kiss the dear fingers, so toilworn
for me,
Oh, God bless you and keep you,
Mother Machree.

—*Rida Johnson Young*

$\mathcal{I}$t was my mother who fought. Fought! To keep me up to par! To make me study and improve. Fought! To keep my name in the large type she thought I merited. Fought for heat in trains to protect my health. Fought to make ends meet, when each week she had finished sending money to the many dependents that automatically arrived on the high heels of success. Invincible! best describes her.

—*Elsie Janis*

$\mathscr{T}$o describe my mother would be to write about a hurricane in its perfect power.

—*Maya Angelou*

Someone
You Can
Count On ...

$\mathcal{M}$y mother, religious-negro,
proud of
having waded through a
storm, is very obviously,
a sturdy Black bridge that I
crossed over, on.

—*Carolyn M. Rodgers*

$\mathcal{I}$ cannot forget my mother. Though not as sturdy as others, she is my bridge. When I needed to get across, she steadied herself long enough for me to run across safely.

—*Renita Weems*

A mother is the truest friend we have, when trials, heavy and sudden, fall upon us; when friends who rejoice with us in our sunshine, desert us; when troubles thicken around us, still she will cling to us, and endeavor by her kind precepts and counsels to dissipate the clouds of darkness and cause peace to return to our hearts.

— *Washington Irving*

*B*lushing, full of confusion,
I talked with her
about my
worries and the fear in my body.
I fell on her
breast,
and all over again I became
a little girl sobbing
in her
arms at the terror of life.

—Gabriela Mistral, in "Mother"

$\mathcal{M}$other — that was the bank in which we deposited all our hurts and worries.

— *DeWitt Talmage*

To love the tender heart hath
ever fled,
As on its mother's breast
the infant throws
Its sobbing face, and there
in sleep forgets
its woe.

—*Mary Tighe*

$\mathcal{Y}$et from my earliest days she always had all the love and care I needed; I cannot recall that I ever felt she had been inadequate when my demands on her were emotional rather than practical.

—*Jonathan Yardley,*
of his mother

$\mathcal{H}$ow beautiful everything is
arranged by Nature; as
soon as a child enters the world, it finds
a mother ready to take care of it.

—*Jules Michelet*

*W*ho ran to help me when I fell,
And would some pretty
story tell,
Or kiss the place to make it well?
My mother.

—*Ann Taylor*

$\mathcal{G}$od could not be everywhere and
therefore he made mothers.

—*Jewish proverb*

$\mathcal{A}$ mother is a person who if she is not there when you get home from school you wouldn't know how to get your dinner, and you wouldn't feel like eating it anyway.

—*Anonymous*

To her whose heart is my heart's
quiet home,
To my first Love, my Mother,
on whose knee
I learnt love-lore that is not
troublesome

—*Christina Rossetti*

$\mathcal{I}$ wonder why you care so much
about me—no, I don't wonder.
I only accept it as the thing at the back
of all one's life that makes everything
bearable and possible.

—Gertrude Bell,
to her mother

$\mathcal{W}$hat do girls do who haven't any
mothers to help them through
their troubles?"

—*Louisa May Alcott*

$\mathcal{I}$ grow old, old
without you,
Mother, landscape
of my heart.

—*Olga Broumas*

$\mathcal{M}$y mother had a slender, small body, but a large heart—a heart so large that everybody's grief and everybody's joy found welcome in it, and hospitable accommodation.

—*Mark Twain*

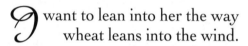

I want to lean into her the way
wheat leans into the wind.

—*Louise Erdrich*

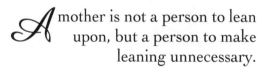

$\mathcal{A}$ mother is not a person to lean upon, but a person to make leaning unnecessary.

—*Dorothy Canfield Fisher*

$\mathcal{M}$ummy herself has told us that she looked upon us more as her friends than her daughters. Now that is all very fine, but still a friend can't take a mother's place. I need my mother as an example which I can follow. I want to be able to respect her.

—*Anne Frank*

*T*he heart of a mother is a deep abyss at the bottom of which you will always discover forgiveness.

—*Honoré de Balzac*

*A*nd it came to me, and I knew what I had to have before my soul would rest. I wanted to belong—to belong to my mother. And in return—I wanted my mother to belong to me.

—*Gloria Vanderbilt*

$\mathcal{M}$other, in ways neither of us
can understand,
I have come home.

—*Robin Morgan*

$\mathcal{M}$other who gave me life
I think of women
bearing
women. Forgive me the wisdom
I would not learn from you.

—*Gwen Harwood*

Yes, a mother is one thing that nobody can do without. And when you have harassed her, buffeted her about, tried her patience, and worn her out, and it seems that the end of the world is about to descend on you, then you can win her back with four little words, "Mom, I love you."

— *William A. Greenbaum II*

*A*h! what a joy is it to be able to turn in full confidence to the one whom we have to thank for our existence.

—*Frederika Bremer*

Backward, flow backward, O Time,
in your flight,
Make me a child again, just for tonight!
Mother, come back from the
echoless shore,
Take me again to your heart, as of yore;
Kiss from my forehead the furrows of care
Smooth the few silver threads
out of my hair,
Over my slumbers your loving
watch keep—
Rock me to sleep, mother, rock me to sleep.

—*Elizabeth Akers Allen*

$\mathcal{S}$he was such a good loving mother, my best friend; oh, who was happier than I when I could still say the dear name "mother," and it was heard, and whom can I say it to now?

—*Ludwig van Beethoven*

*O*f you've ever had a mother, if she's given you and meant to you all the things you care for most, you never get over it.

—*Anne Douglas Sedgwick*

*I*t is clear to me, every little while, that my soul is not big enough to get along without a very personal reason for existence. You will be that person for a long, *long* time yet. Won't you?

—*Crystal Eastman,*
to her mother, Annis Ford Eastman

Hundreds of dewdrops to
greet the dawn;
Hundreds of lambs in the
purple clover;
Hundreds of butterflies
on the lawn;
But only one mother the
wide world over.

— *George Cooper*

$\mathcal{M}$ost of all the other beautiful things in life come by twos and threes, by dozens and by hundreds. Plenty of roses, stars, sunsets, rainbows, brothers and sisters, aunts and cousins, comrades and friends—but only one mother in the whole world.

—*Kate Douglas Wiggin*

$\mathcal{A}$ mother's love for her child is like nothing else in the world. It knows no law, no pity, it dares all things and crushes down remorselessly all that stands in its path.

—*Agatha Christie*

$\mathcal{A}$ mother is she who can take the place of all others, but whose place no one else can take.

—*Cardinal Mermil*

$\mathcal{J}$ust as breast milk cannot be
duplicated, neither
can a mother.

—*Sally E. Shaywitz*

There is none,
In all this
cold and hollow world, no fount
Of deep, strong, deathless love, save
that within
A mother's heart.

—*Felicia Hemans*

$\mathcal{I}$'ve got more children than I can rightly take care of, but I ain't got more than I can love.

—*Ossie Guffy*

There is nothing so strong as the force of love; there is no love so forcible as the love of an affectionate mother to her natural child.

—*Elizabeth Grymeston,
in a letter to her son*

$\mathcal{W}$omanliness means only
motherhood;
And love begins and ends
there — roams enough,
But, having run the circle,
rests at home.

—*Robert Browning*

When you are dead your sister's tears will dry as time goes on, your widow's tears will cease in another's arms, but your mother will mourn you till the day she dies.

—*Arab proverb*

$\mathcal{N}$o one had told her what it would be like, the way she loved her children. What a thing of the body it was, as physically rooted as sexual desire, but without its edge of danger.

—*Mary Gordon*

$\mathcal{A}$ll the earth, though it were full of
kind hearts, is but a desolation
and a desert place to a mother when her
only child is absent.

—*Elizabeth Gaskell*

*Y*outh fades; love droops; the
leaves of
friendship fall:
A mother's secret outlives them all.

—*Oliver Wendell Holmes*

$\mathcal{I}$ cannot consent to be separated
from my son. I can feel no
enjoyment without my children; with
them I can regret nothing.

—*Marie Antoinette*

$\mathcal{L}$ove twisted suddenly . . . inside her, compelling her to reach into the crib and lift up the moist, breathing weight. . . . The smells of baby powder and clean skin and warm flannel mingled with a sharp scent of wet nappy.

—*Rosie Thomas*

What are Raphael's Madonnas but
the shadow of a mother's love,
fixed in permanent outline forever.

— *Thomas Wentworth Higginson*

$\mathcal{Y}$ou never get over bein' a child as
long's you have a mother
to go to.

—*Sarah Orne Jewett*

$\mathcal{A}$h, lucky girls who grow up in the shelter of a mother's love—a mother who knows how to contrive opportunities without conceding favors, how to take advantage of propinquity without allowing appetite to be dulled by habit.

—*Edith Wharton*

$\mathcal{A}$ mother's hardest to forgive.
Life is the fruit she longs to
hand you,
Ripe on a plate. And while you live,
Relentlessly she understands you.

—*Phyllis McGinley*

$\mathcal{M}$other's love grows by giving.

—*Charles Lamb*

*A*lways that tyrannical love reaches out. Soft words shrivel me like quicklime. She will not allow me to be cold, hungry. She will insist that I take her own coat, her own food.

—*Elizabeth Smart*

*O*h, what a power is motherhood,
                          possessing
A potent spell. All women alike
      Fight fiercely for a child.

—Euripides

*S*he had risen and was walking
about the room, her fat, worn
face sharpening with a sort of animal
alertness into power and protection. The
claws that hide in every maternal
creature slipped out of the
fur of good manners.

—*Margaret Deland*

There was a place in childhood,
that I remember well,
And there a voice of sweetest tone, fairy
tales did tell,
And gentle words, and fond embrace,
were given with joy to me,
When I was in that happy place upon
my mother's knee.

—*Samuel Lover*

Who takes the child by the hand
takes the mother by the heart.

—*Danish proverb*

$\mathcal{J}$f I get the forty additional years statisticians say are likely coming to me, I could fit in at least one, maybe two new lifetimes. Sad that only one of those lifetimes can include being the mother of young children.

—*Anna Quindlen*

$\mathcal{W}$hen people inquire I always
just state,
"I have four nice children, and
hope to have eight."

—*Aline Murray Kilmer,*
in "Ambition"

*H*ere's what I taught my daughters:
Become women of substance.
Work for yourselves if you can. That way
you won't have to take any lip, and you
can work the hours you want. Never buy
artificial fabric; always buy silk. If you can
save any money, buy your own place, and
keep it in your name. . . . And if you hate
to save, or be tied down, put your money
in jewelry. Even if it's only garnets or jade,
it's yours, and it's wealth. And never,
never do a job if it isn't fun.

— *Carolyn See*

$\mathcal{T}$he mother loves her child most divinely, not when she surrounds him with comfort and anticipates his wants, but when she resolutely holds him to the highest standards and is content with nothing less than his best.

—*Hamilton Wright Mabie*

$\mathscr{E}$very beetle is a gazelle in the eyes
of its mother.

—Moorish proverb

$\mathcal{A}$ mother . . . is forever surprised and even faintly wronged that her sons and daughters are just people, for many mothers hope and half expect that their newborn child will make the world better, will somehow be a redeemer. Perhaps they are right, and they can believe that the rare quality they glimpsed in the child is active in the unburdened adult.

—*Florida Scott-Maxwell*

Integral to being emotionally healthy is to have a mother who has the ability to respect her child's differences and not perceive them as betrayals. A good mother can allow her child to be less than perfect.

— *Victoria Secunda*

$\mathcal{N}$o matter how old a mother is, she watches her middle-aged children for signs of improvement.

—*Florida Scott-Maxwell*

Did you ever meet a mother who's complained that her child phoned her too often? Me neither.

—*Maureen Lipman*

*B*ut the actual power a woman has
is to make a group of people
happy and make them grow in the right
way and contribute to the world.
Knowing that you release your family
into the day with your love and with
your warmth is the richness of life.

—*Maria Schell*

When I held you, Jane — my first baby — in my arms, I had the greatest thrill I have ever experienced.

—*Mrs. Colbert,*
to her daughter

*O*nly a mother knows a
mother's fondness.

—*Lady Mary Wortley Montagu*

If I were hanged on the highest hill,
    Mother o' mine, O mother
        o' mine!
    I know whose love would
        follow me still,
    Mother o' mine, O mother
        o' mine!

—*Rudyard Kipling*

For the entire five years of my son's life, I have been preparing him to worship the ground I walk on. To date, my crusade hasn't even gotten him to bend a knee.

—*Claudette Russel*

$\mathcal{S}$ome are kissing mothers and some are scolding mothers, but it is love just the same, and most mothers kiss and scold together.

—*Pearl S. Buck*

$\mathcal{N}$o mother wants to let go.

—*Anthony Burgess*

There is a sensation in a mother's breast at the loss of an infant that partakes of the feeling of instinct. It is a species of savage despair.

—*Elizabeth Holland*

$\mathcal{Y}$ears to a mother bring distress
But do not make her
love the less.

— *William Wordsworth*

$\mathcal{F}$or that's what a woman, a mother wants—to teach her children to take an interest in life. She knows it's safer for them to be interested in other people's happiness than to believe in their own.

—*Marguerite Duras*

$\mathcal{L}$oving a child doesn't mean giving in to all his whims; to love him is to bring out the best in him, to teach him to love what is difficult.

—*Nadia Boulanger*

MOTHER: Do you love me, Albert?
ALBERT: Yes.
MOTHER: Yes—what?
ALBERT: Yes, please.

—Tom Stoppard

*M*others may still want their favorite sons to grow up to be President, but, according to a famous Gallup poll of some years ago, they do not want them to become politicians in the process.

—*John F. Kennedy*

$\mathcal{T}$his is a moment I deeply wished my parents could have lived to share. In the first place my father would have enjoyed what you have so generously said of me—and my mother would have believed it.

—*Lyndon B. Johnson*

A dvice to mothers: Take off your earrings, your ring, your precious family heirloom, and give it to [your daughter] along with your love and trust. Trust and love are wonderful, but don't forget the earrings.

—*Estée Lauder*

*B*efore becoming a mother I had a hundred theories on how to bring up children. Now I have seven children and one theory: love them, especially when they least deserve to be loved.

—*Kate Samperi*

$\mathcal{W}$hat I most wanted for my daughter was that she be able to soar confidently *in her own sky,* wherever that might be, and if there was space for me as well I would, indeed, have reaped what I had tried to sow.

—*Helen Claes*

A mother has, perhaps, the hardest earthly lot; and yet no mother worthy of the name ever gave herself thoroughly for her child who did not feel that, after all, she reaped what she had sown.

—*Henry Ward Beecher*

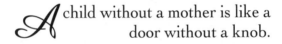

$\mathcal{A}$ child without a mother is like a
door without a knob.

—*Jewish proverb*

$\mathcal{R}$omance fails us — and so do friendships — but the relationship of Mother and Child remains indelible and indestructible — the strongest bond upon this earth.

— *Theodore Reik*

$\mathcal{O}$h, the unhappy people who have not you for a mother! My heart goes out to them . . .

—*Crystal Eastman,*
to her mother, Annis Ford Eastman

Women know
The way to
rear up children (to be just),
They know a simple, merry,
tender knack
Of tying sashes, fitting baby shoes,
And stringing pretty words
that make no
sense.

—*Elizabeth Barrett Browning*

We *need* each other. I'm glad the tho't of me so often helps you—it is because I am not too near—you forget my fatal weakness and only know my love and my aching desire to be *with you where you are* in all the heights and depths.

—*Annis Ford Eastman,*
to her daughter, Crystal

$\mathcal{W}$hen you are a mother, you are never really alone in your thoughts. You are connected to your child and to all those who touch your lives. A mother always has to think twice, one for herself and once for her child.

—*Sophia Loren*

$\mathcal{M}$otherhood has been the most joyous and important experience in my life. I would die for my children.

—*Carly Simon*

$\mathcal{W}$hat I think I have in common
with every mother on the
face of the earth is the primacy of one's
children in one's life—that they're
everything in some bizarre way.

—*Jane Silverman*

$\mathscr{B}$lest the babe,
Nursed in
his mother's arms,
who sucks to sleep
Pocked on his mother's breast,
who with his soul
Drink in the feelings of
his mother's eye!

— *William Wordsworth*

To talk to a child, to fascinate him, is much more difficult than to win an electoral victory. But it is more rewarding.

—*Colette*

*Y*our happiness was my first wish, and the pursuit of all my actions, divested of all self-interest. So far I think you ought, and believe you do, remember me as your real friend.

—*Lady Mary Wortley Montagu,*
to her daughter

Her
Influence

$\mathcal{T}$here is no influence so powerful
as that of the mother.

—*Sarah Josepha Hale*

$\mathcal{W}$omen as the guardians of children possess a great power. They are the molders of their children's personalities and the arbiters of their development.

—Ann Oakley

$\mathcal{I}$ learned your walk, talk, gestures and nurturing laughter. At that time, Mama, had you swung from bars, I would, to this day, be hopelessly, imitatively, hung up.

—*SDiane Bogus*

$\mathcal{M}$others of the race, the most
important actors
in the grand drama of the
human progress . . .

—*Elizabeth Cady Stanton*

*A*dmitting that it is the profession of our sex to teach, we perceive the mother to be first in point of precedence, in degree of power, in the faculty of teaching, and in the department allotted. For in point of precedence she is next to the Creator; in power over her pupil, limitless and without competitor; in faculty of teaching, endowed with the prerogative of a transforming love; while the glorious department allotted is a newly quickened soul and its immortal destiny.

—*Lydia Howard Sigourney*

O wondrous power! how
little understood,
Entrusted to the mother's mind alone
To fashion genius, from the
soul for good,
Inspire a West, or train
a Washington!

—*Sarah Josepha Hale*

$\mathcal{Y}$ou may have tangible
wealth untold;
Caskets of jewels and
coffers of gold.
Richer than I you can never be—
I had a mother who read to me.

—*Strickland Gillilan*

$\mathcal{W}$hat the mother sings to the
cradle goes all the way
down to the coffin.

—Henry Ward Beecher

They say that man is mighty,
  He governs land and sea,
He wields a mighty scepter
O'er lesser powers that be;
But a mightier power and stronger
Man from his throne has hurled,
For the hand that rocks the cradle
Is the hand that rules the world.

— *William Ross Wallace*

$\mathcal{T}$he future destiny of the child is
always the work
of the mother.

—*Napoleon Bonaparte I*

$\mathcal{A}$ man never sees all that his mother has been to him till it's too late to let her know that he sees it.

— *William Dean Howells*

$\mathcal{I}$ find, by close observation, that the mothers are the levers which move in education. The men talk about it . . . but the women work for it.

—*Frances Watkins Harper*

$\mathcal{I}$ opine . . . "Judicious mothers will always keep in mind, that they are the first book read, and the last put aside, in every child's library."

—*C. Lenox Remond*

To many a mother's heart has come the disappointment of a loss of power, a limitation of influence when early manhood takes the boy from the home, or when even before that time, in school, or where he touches the great world and begins to be bewildered with its controversies, trade and economics and politics make their imprint even while his lips are dewy with his mother's kiss.

—*J. Ellen Foster*

It is a general rule that all superior
men inherit the elements of
superiority from their mothers.

—*Jules Michelet*

$\mathcal{H}$appier he
With
such a mother! faith in womankind
Beats with his blood, and trust in all
things high
Comes easy to him, and tho'
he trip and fall
He shall not bind his soul with clay.

—Alfred, Lord Tennyson

$\mathcal{T}$he students of history know that while many mothers of great men have been virtuous, none have been commonplace, and few have been happy.

—*Gertrude Atherton*

$\mathcal{M}$en are what their mothers
made them.

—*Ralph Waldo Emerson*

$\mathcal{L}$et France have good mothers and
she will have good sons.

—Napoleon Bonaparte I

$\mathcal{T}$he only time a woman really
succeeds in changing a man
is when he is a baby.

—*Natalie Wood*

$\mathcal{I}$ can't help it. I like things clean.
Blame it on my mother. I was
toilet trained at five months old.

—*Neil Simon*

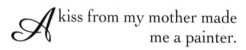

$\mathcal{A}$ kiss from my mother made
me a painter.

—*Benjamin West*

$\mathcal{A}$ man who has been the
indisputable favorite
of his mother keeps for life the feeling of
a conqueror, that confidence of success
that often induces real success.

—*Sigmund Freud*

So when the great word
"Mother!" rang once
more,
I saw at last its meaning and its place;
Not the blind passion of the
brooding past,
But Mother—the World's
Mother—come at
last,
To love as she had never loved before—
To feed and guard and teach the
human race.

—*Charlotte Perkins Gilman*

We bear the world, and we make it.
. . . There was never a great man
who had not a great mother—it is
hardly an exaggeration.

—*Olive Schreiner*

When we see great men and women, we give credit to their mothers. When we see inferior men and women—and that is a common circumstance—no one presumes to the question of the motherhood which has produced them.

—*Charlotte Perkins Gilman*

$\mathcal{M}$others who have little sense of their own minds and voices are unable to imagine such capacities in their children. Not being fully aware of the power of words for communicating meaning, they expect their children to know what is on their minds without the benefit of words. These parents do not tell their children what they mean by "good," much less why. Nor do they ask the children to explain themselves.

—*Mary Field Belenky*

*A*nd say to mothers what
a holy charge
Is theirs —with what a kingly
power their
love
Might rule the fountains of
the new-born
mind.

—*Lydia Howard Sigourney*

Examine the personality of the mother, who is the medium through which the primitive infant transforms himself into a socialized human being.

—*Beata Rank*

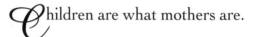

Children are what mothers are.

— *Walter Savage Landor*

The child craves of the mother, the work craves of its creator: the vision, the waiting, the hope, the pure will, the faith, and the love; the power to suffer, the desire to sacrifice, the ecstasy of devotion. Thus, man also has his "motherliness," a compound of feelings corresponding to those with which the woman enriches the race, oftener than the work, but which in woman, as in man, constitutes the productive mental process without which neither new works nor new generations turn out well.

—*Ellen Key*

$\mathcal{T}$hat best academy, a
mother's knee.

—*James Russell Lowell*

$\mathcal{T}$o say nothing of that brief but despotic sway which every woman possesses over the man in love with her—a power immense, unaccountable, invaluable; but in general so evanescent as but to make a brilliant episode in the tale of life—how almost immeasurable is the influence exercised by sisters, friends, and, most of all, by mothers!

—*Anne Marsh*

he mother's face and voice are the
first conscious objects the infant
soul unfolds, and she soon comes to
stand in the very place of God
to her child.

—*Granville Stanley Hall*

$\mathcal{M}$y mother is a poem I'll never be
able to write
though everything I write is a poem to
my mother.

—*Sharon Doubiago*

𝒴ours the voice
Sounding
ever in my ears.

—*Madeline Mason-Manheim,*
in "To My Mother"

$\mathcal{I}$know her face by heart. Sometimes
I think nothing will break
her spell.

—*Daphne Merkin*

sharpen more and more to your
     Likeness every year.

—*Michelle Wolf,*
in "For My Mother"

The mother's heart is the child's schoolroom.

—*Henry Ward Beecher*

$\mathcal{I}$ am a reflection of my mother's secret poetry as well as of her hidden angers.

—*Audre Lorde*

A woman *is* her mother.
That's the main thing.

—*Anne Sexton*

i am not you anymore
i am my own
collection of
gifts and errors.

—*Saundra Sharp*

*I*n search of my mother's
garden, I found
my own.

—*Alice Walker*

*I*nstant availability without continuous presence is probably the best role a mother can play.

—*Lotte Bailyn*

$\mathscr{A}$ mother starts out as the most important person in her child's world and if she's successful in her work, she will eventually become the stupidest.

—*Mary Kay Blakely*

*O*h, to be half as wonderful as my child thought I was when he was small, and only half as stupid as my teenager thinks I am.

—*Rebecca Richards*

$\mathcal{T}$he most universal of truisms is that we all have had a mother. However long or brief that relationship, and however good or bad, there is no disputing that the quality of that relationship is central to our being.

—*Emily Rosen*

*t*reetalk and windsong are
the language of my
mother
her music does not leave me.

— *Barbara Mahone*

$\mathcal{N}$o woman can shake off her
mother. There should be
no mothers, only women.

—*George Bernard Shaw*

$\mathcal{N}$o song or poem will bear my mother's name. Yet so many of the stories that I write, that we all write, are my mother's stories.

—*Alice Walker*

*M*y mother had died when I was seven. For many years I lived primarily to search for her.

—*Jane Lazarre*

$\mathcal{T}$he longer one lives in this hard world motherless, the more a mother's loss makes itself felt.

—*Jane Welsh Carlyle*

$\mathcal{T}$he death of my mother
permanently affects
my happiness, more even than I should
have anticipated. . . . I did not
apprehend, during her life, to what a
degree she prevented me from feeling
heart-solitude.

—*Sara Coleridge*

What I object to in Mother is that she wants me to think her thoughts. Apart from the question of hypocrisy, I prefer my own.

—*Margaret Deland*

I fear, as any daughter would, losing myself back into the mother.

—*Kim Chernin*

*O*h! mothers aren't fair — I mean it's not fair of nature to weigh us down with them and yet expect us to be our own true selves. The handicap's too great. All those months, when the same blood's running through two sets of veins — there's no getting away from that ever after.

—*Henry Handel Richardson*

$\mathcal{O}$ut of the corner of one eye, I could see my mother. Out of the corner of the other eye, I could see her shadow on the wall, cast there by the lamplight. It was a big and solid shadow, and it looked so much like my mother that I became frightened. For I could not be sure whether for the rest of my life I would be able to tell when it was really my mother and when it was really her shadow standing between me and the rest of the world.

—*Jamaica Kincaid*

$\mathcal{I}$n the final analysis, each of us is responsible for what we are. We cannot blame it on our mothers, who thanks to Freud, have replaced money as the root of all evil.

—*Helen Lawerson*

Sometimes we blame Mom too much for all that is wrong with her sons and daughters. After all, we might well ask, who started the grim mess? Who long ago made Mom and her sex "inferior" and stripped her of her economic and political and sexual rights? . . . Man, born of woman, has found it a hard thing to forgive her for giving him birth. The patriarchal protest against the ancient matriarch has borne strange fruit through the years.

—*Lillian Smith*

*F*ashions change, and with the new psychoanalytical perspective of the postwar period [WWII], child rearing became enshrined as the special responsibility of mothers. . . . Any shortcoming in adult life was now seen as rooted in the failure of mothering during childhood.

—*Sylvia Ann Hewlett*

"*Mother*" is the first word that occurs to politicians and columnists and popes when they raise the question, "Why isn't life turning out the way we wanted it?"

—*Mary Kay Blakely*

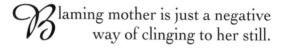

*B*laming mother is just a negative
way of clinging to her still.

—*Nancy Friday*

When the strongest words for
what I have to offer come
out of me sounding like words I
remember from my mother's mouth,
then I have to reassess the meaning of
everything I have to say now, or
re-examine the worth of her old words.

—*Audre Lorde*

*E*ven though fathers, grandparents, siblings, memories of ancestors are important agents of socialization, our society focuses on the attributes and characteristics of mothers and teachers and gives them the ultimate responsibility for the child's life chances.

—*Sara Lawrence Lightfoot*

I think most women are scared to death, because we are molding and influencing the most important thing we have ever created, our children. So here we are, sailing out into these totally uncharted waters. And for someone like me, who was trying and wanting to be the best at everything, there were a lot of anxious, anxious moments.

—*Ann Richards*

$\mathcal{T}$he walks and talks we have with
our two-year-olds in red boots
have a great deal to do with the values
they will cherish as adults.

—*Edith F. Hunter*

Having Children

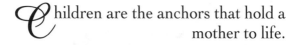

$\mathcal{C}$hildren are the anchors that hold a
mother to life.

—*Sophocles*

$\mathcal{T}$here is no other closeness in human life like the closeness between a mother and her baby—chronologically, physically, and spiritually they are just a few heartbeats away from being the same person.

—*Susan Cheever*

We are together, my child and I.
Mother and child, yes, but
sisters really, against whatever denies us
all that we are.

—*Alice Walker*

You might not have thought it possible to give birth to others before one has given birth to oneself, but I assure you it is quite possible, it has been done; I offer myself in evidence as Exhibit A.

—*Sheila Ballantyne*

*P*regnancy doubled her, birth
halved her, and
motherhood turned her into
Everywoman.

—*Erica Jong*

With two sons born eighteen months apart, I operated mainly on automatic pilot through the ceaseless activity of their early childhood. I remember opening the refrigerator late one night and finding a roll of aluminum foil next to a pair of small red tennies. Certain that I was responsible for the refrigerated shoes, I quickly closed the door and ran upstairs to make sure I had put the babies in their cribs instead of the linen closet.

—*Mary Kay Blakely*

This is the reason why mothers are more devoted to their children than fathers: it is that they suffer more in giving them birth and are more certain that they are their own.

—*Aristotle*

I begin to love this little creature, and to anticipate his birth as a fresh twist to a knot, which I do not wish to untie.

—*Mary Wollstonecraft*

$\mathcal{I}$ think carrying a baby inside of you is like running as fast as you can. It feels like finally letting go and filling yourself up to the widest limits.

—*Anonymous*

$\mathcal{B}$ecause humans are not alone in exhibiting such behaviors—bees stockpile royal jelly, birds feather their nests, mice shred paper—it's possible that a pregnant woman who scrubs her house from floor to ceiling [just before her baby is born] is responding to a biological imperative. . . . Of course there are those who believe that . . . the burst of energy that propels a pregnant woman to clean her house is a perfectly natural response to their mother's impending visit.

—*Mary Arrigo*

When a woman is twenty, a child deforms her; when she is thirty, he preserves her; and when forty, he makes her young again.

—*Léon Blum*

$\mathcal{I}$n the mind of a woman, to give
  birth to a child is the shortcut
            to omniscience.

                    — *Gelett Burgess*

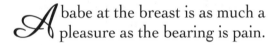

A babe at the breast is as much a
pleasure as the bearing is pain.

—*Marion Zimmer Bradley*

If you want to know the feeling [of labor pain], just take your bottom lip and pull it over your head.

— *Carol Burnett*

*I*f pregnancy were a book they
would cut out the last
two chapters.

—*Nora Ephron*

The frequency of personal questions grows in direct proportion to your increasing girth. . . . No one would ask a man such a personally invasive question as "Is your wife having natural childbirth or is she planning to be knocked out?" But someone might ask that of you. No matter how much you wish for privacy, your pregnancy is a public event to which everyone feels invited.

—*Jean Marzollo*

$\mathcal{N}$ow that I'm pregnant I feel
beautiful for the first time
in my life.

—*Karen Alexander*

*I*n the sheltered simplicity of the
first days after a baby is born,
one sees again the magical closed circle,
the miraculous sense of two people
existing only for each other.

—*Anne Morrow Lindbergh*

$\mathcal{W}$hen a child enters the world
through you, it alters
everything on a psychic, physiological
and purely practical level.

—*Jane Fonda*

$\mathcal{L}$ife is the first gift, love is the
second, understanding
the third.

—*Marge Piercy*

*O*h, mine was as rosy as a bough
　　Blooming with roses, sent,
　　　　somehow,
　　　　To bloom for me!
His balmy fingers left a thrill
Deep in my breast that warms me still.

—*Agnes Lee,*
"Motherhood"

$\mathcal{M}$y darling little girl-child, after such a long and troublesome waiting I now have you in my arms. I am alone no more. I have my baby.

—Martha Martin

$\mathcal{I}$ stood in the hospital corridor the night after she was born. Through a window I could see all the small, crying newborn infants and somewhere among them was the one who was mine. I stood there for hours filled with happiness until the night nurse sent me to bed.

—*Liv Ullman*

I actually remember feeling delight,
at two o'clock in the morning,
when the baby woke for his feed,
because I so longed to have
another look at him.

—*Margaret Drabble*

$\mathcal{W}$ho is getting more pleasure from
this rocking, the baby or me?

—*Nancy Thayer*

I saw pure love when my son looked at me, and I knew that I had made a good life for the two of us . . .

—*Suzanne Somers*

$\mathcal{I}$t is the biggest gamble in the world. It is the glorious life force. It's huge and scary—it's an act of infinite optimism.

—*Gilda Radner,*
on having children

$\mathcal{I}$ remember leaving the hospital . . .
thinking, "Wait, are they going to
let me just walk off with him? I don't
know beans about babies! I don't have a
license to do this. [We're]
just amateurs."

—*Anne Tyler*

I have always felt that too much time was given before birth, which is spent learning things like how to breathe in and out with your husband (I had my baby when they gave you a shot in the hip and you didn't wake up until the kid was ready to start school), and not enough time given to how to mother after the baby is born.

—*Erma Bombeck*

$\mathcal{L}$ife was diapers and little jars of
puréed apricots and bottles
and playpens and rectal thermometers,
and all those small dirty faces and all
those questions.

—*Pat Loud*

"You agreed to get up nights."
This is true. I stumble into
the nursery, pick up my son,
so small, so perfect, and as he fastens
himself to me like a tiny, suckling
minnow I am flooded with tenderness.

—*Sara Davidson*

While you can quarrel with a grown-up, how can you quarrel with a newborn baby who has stretched out his little arms for you to pick him up?

—Maria von Trapp

If enforced wakefulness is the handmaiden and necessary precursor to serious brainwashing, a mother—after her first child—is ready for her final demise.

—*Beverly Jones*

Life is crazy. Now, maybe you knew this all along. But before I had children, I actually held on to the illusion that there was some sense of order in the universe. . . . I am now convinced that we are all living in a Chagall painting—a world where brides and grooms and cows and chickens and angels and sneakers are all mixed up together, sometimes floating in the air, sometimes upside down and everywhere.

—*Susan Lapinski*

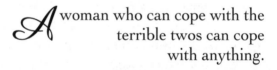

A woman who can cope with the
terrible twos can cope
with anything.

—*Judith Clabes*

*E*very nursing mother, in the midst of her little dependent brood, has far more right to whine, sulk, or scold, as temperament dictates, because beefsteak and coffee are not prepared for her and exactly to her taste, than any man ever had or ever can have during the present stage of human evolution.

—*Antoinette Brown Blackwell*

$\mathcal{I}$'ve become a mother. That's why women grow up and men don't.

—*Kathleen Cleaver*

*E*very woman should have a child. The sense of loss must be painful to those without a maternal relationship. You complete the full range of emotions. For me, that's what living is all about.

—*Donna Karan*

$\mathcal{T}$he commonest fallacy among women is that simply having children makes one a mother—which is as absurd as believing that having a piano makes one a musician.

—*Syòney J. Harris*

*A*lthough there are many trial
marriages . . . there is no
such thing as a trial child.

—*Gail Sheehy*

*Y*ou can't change your mind—you know, and say, this isn't working out, let's sell.

—*Fran Lebowitz,*
on having children

*M*any times married women desire children, as maids do husbands, more for honour than for comfort or happiness, thinking it a disgrace to live old maids, and so likewise to be barren.

—*Margaret Cavendish*

$\mathcal{M}$aking the decision to have a
child—it's momentous.
It is to decide forever to have your heart
go walking around outside your body.

—*Elizabeth Stone*

$\mathcal{T}$o have a son in wartime is the worst curse that can befall a mother, no matter what anyone says.

—*Slavenka Drakulíc*

$\mathcal{F}$ive years ago I thought the most courageous thing was not to get married, not to have children. That all seemed so predictable and safe. Now I think the most courageous thing is to get married and *have* children, because that seems the most worthwhile.

—*Candice Bergen*

$\mathcal{T}$he gain is not the having of children; it is the discovery of love and how to be loving.

— *Polly Berrien Berends*

There is nothing more thrilling in this world, I think, than having a child that is yours, and yet is mysteriously a stranger.

—*Agatha Christie*

*G*ood mothers know that their
relationship with each of
their children is like a
moveable feast, constantly
changing and evolving.

—*Sue Woodman*

*O*f you bungle raising your children,
I don't think whatever else you do
well matters very much.

—*Jacqueline Kennedy Onassis*

$\mathcal{W}$hen people ask me what I do, I always say I am a mother first. Your children represent your thoughts. Your children are a statement.

—*Jacqueline Johnson*

I used to be a reasonably careless and adventurous person before I had children; now I am morbidly obsessed by seat-belts and constantly afraid that low-flying aircraft will drop on my children's school.

—*Margaret Drabble*

$\mathcal{I}$f you want your children to turn out well, spend twice as much time with them, and half as much money.

—*Abigail Van Buren*

$\mathcal{N}$othing else will make you as
happy or as sad, as proud
or as tired, for nothing is quite as hard
as helping a person develop his own
individuality—especially while you
struggle to keep your own.

—*Marguerite Kelly and Elia Parsons*

*O*h, what a power is motherhood,
                  possessing
A potent spell. All women alike
      Fight fiercely for a child.

—Euripides

$\mathcal{L}$ove them, feed them, discipline
them and let them go free.
You may have a lifelong relationship.

—*Mary G. L. Davis*

$\mathscr{T}$he successful mother sets her children free and becomes more free herself in the process.

—*Robert J. Hauighurst*

$\mathcal{F}$inally, simply, if I hadn't had a child, I'd never have known that most elemental, direct, true relationship. I don't know if I'd fully understand the values of society that I prize. I would have missed some of the mystery of life and death. Not to know how a child grows, the wonder of a newborn's hand . . . I have been fortunate.

—*Dianne Feinstein*

$\mathcal{W}$hen she [her daughter] comes and looks in my face and calls me "mother," indeed I then truly am a mother.

—*Emma Hamilton*

Being a Mother

$\mathcal{I}$ love being a mother . . . I am more
aware. I feel things on a deeper
level. I have a kind of understanding
about my body, about being a woman.

—*Shelley Long*

$\mathcal{B}$iology is the least of what makes
someone a mother.

—*Oprah Winfrey*

$\mathcal{T}$here's a lot more to being a woman than being a mother, but there's a hell of a lot more to being a mother than most people suspect.

—*Roseanne*

$\mathcal{W}$oman, Mother—your
responsibility is one
that might make angels tremble fear to
take hold.

—*Anna Julia Cooper*

*M*others had a thousand thoughts
    to get through within a day,
and . . . most of these were about
            avoiding disaster.

—*Natalie Kusz*

$\mathcal{I}$t's the biggest on-the-job training
program in existence today.

—*Erma Bombeck,*
on being a mother

$\mathcal{T}$ruth, which is important to a scholar, has got to be concrete. And there is nothing more concrete than dealing with babies, burps and bottles, frogs and mud.

—*Jeanne J. Kirkpatrick*

$\mathcal{M}$ost mothers are instinctive
philosophers.

—*Harriet Beecher Stowe*

*H*ence the spiritual weariness of
the conscientious mother:
you're always finding out just one
more vital tidbit.

—*Sonia Taitz*

$\mathcal{M}$others are the only race of people that speak the same tongue. A mother in Manchuria could converse with a mother in Nebraska and never miss a word.

— *Will Rogers*

$\mathcal{W}$omen—wives and mothers—are
the same everywhere.

—*Mary Boykin Chesnut*

*M*others are not the nameless, faceless stereotypes who appear once a year on a greeting card with their virtues set in prose, but women who have been dealt a hand for life and play each card one at a time the best way they know how. No mother is all good or all bad, all laughing or all serious, all loving or all angry. Ambivalence rushes through their veins.

—*Erma Bombeck*

*B*ecause I am a mother, I am capable of being shocked; as I never was when I was not one.

—*Margaret Atwood*

$\mathcal{B}$eing a full-time mother is one of the highest salaried jobs in my field, since the payment is pure love.

—*Mildred B. Vermont*

$\mathcal{I}$'m living proof it's possible to flunk
Home Ec, as I did in the eighth
grade, and still be an
outstanding mother.

—*Pat Collins*

$\mathcal{B}$eing a "good mother" does not call for the same qualities as being a "good" housewife, and the pressure to be both at the same time may be an insupportable burden.

—*Ann Oakley*

*B*eing a housewife and a mother is the biggest job in the world, but if it doesn't interest you, don't do it. Anyway, I would have made a terrible parent. The first time my child didn't do what I wanted, I'd kill him.

—*Katharine Hepburn*

$\mathscr{T}$he art of living is to function in
society without doing violence
to one's own needs or to the needs of
others. The art of mothering is to teach
the art of living to children.

—*Elaine Heffner*

$\mathcal{W}$omen find ways to give sense
and meaning to daily life —
ways to be useful in the community, to
keep mind active and soul growing even
while they change diapers and
cook vegetables.

—*Lillian Breslow Rubin*

$\mathscr{B}$eing a mother, as far as I can tell, is a constantly evolving process of adapting to the needs of your child while also changing and growing as a person in your own right.

—*Deborah Insel*

$\mathcal{M}$others . . . are basically a patient
lot. They have to be or they
would devour their offspring early on,
like guppies.

—*Mary Daheim*

$\mathcal{N}$o ordinary work done by man is neither as hard or as responsible as the work of a woman who is bringing up a family of small children; for upon her time and strength demands are made not only every hour of the day but often every hour of the night.

— *Theodore Roosevelt*

*O*ne moment makes a father,
  but a mother
Is made by endless moments,
  load on load.

—*John G. Neihardt*

$\mathcal{I}$t's not easy being a mother. If it were fathers would do it.

Bea Arthur,
playing Dorothy in The Golden Girls

$\mathcal{T}$he only difference between men and women is that women are able to create new little human beings in their bodies while simultaneously writing books, driving tractors, working in offices, planting crops — in general doing everything that men do.

—*Erica Jong*

$\mathcal{I}$f evolution really works, how come mothers still have only two hands?

—*Ed Dussault*

$\mathcal{N}$ow, as always, the most
automated appliance in
a household is the mother.

—*Beverly Jones*

$\mathcal{M}$ost days I feel like an acrobat high above a crowd out of which my own parents, my in-laws, potential employers, phantoms of "other women who do it" and a thousand faceless eyes stare up.

—*Anonymous*

$\mathcal{I}$ know how to do anything—
I'm a mom.

—*Roseanne*

 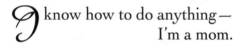 365 REFLECTIONS ON MOTHERS

As Kids Grow Up

One of the things I've discovered in general about raising kids is that they really don't give a damn if you walked five miles to school. They deal with what's happening now.

—*Patty Duke*

The easiest way to convince my children that they don't need anything is to get it for them.

—*Joan Collins*

$\mathcal{D}$o not, on a rainy day, ask your child what he feels like doing, because I assure you that what he feels like doing, you won't feel like watching.

—*Fran Lebowitz*

$\mathcal{C}$leaning your house while your
kids are still growing is like
shoveling the walk before it
stops snowing.

—*Phyllis Diller*

$\mathcal{T}$he darn trouble with cleaning the house is it gets dirty the next day anyway, so skip a week if you have to. The children are the most important thing.

—*Barbara Bush*

$\mathcal{T}$rivial things and important things wound into and against one another, all warring for her attention. Changing the goldfish water wasn't vital, but it couldn't wait. . . . Listening to [the children], growing with them, that was vital; but the bills had to be paid now, the dinner was burning right now.

—*Joanne Greenberg*

$\mathcal{I}$ figure when my husband comes home from work, if the kids are still alive, then I've done my job.

—*Roseanne*

$\mathcal{T}$here is no prescribed method for resolving every specific conflict a mother has with her child, and there is certainly no method that will enable her to have exactly what she wants. . . . There is, however, a larger goal, which is to establish an overall climate of reasonableness, one in which she and her child can hear each other.

—*Elaine Heffner*

$\mathcal{I}$f there were no schools to take children away from home part of the time, the insane asylums would be filled with mothers.

—*E. W. Howe*

A suburban mother's role is to
deliver children
obstetrically once, and
by car ever after.

—*Peter de Vries*

$\mathcal{N}$ever lend your car to anyone to
whom you have given birth.

—*Erma Bombeck*

A mother is never cocky or proud, because she knows the school principal may call at any minute to report that her child has just driven a motorcycle through the gymnasium.

—*Mary Kay Blakely*

I always brought up my children not
to believe in Mother's Day gifts,
and now I regret it.

—*Lauren Bacall*

Motherhood

$\mathcal{M}$otherhood is the second oldest profession in the world. It never questions age, height, religious preference, health, political affiliation, citizenship, morality, ethnic background, marital status, economic level, convenience, or previous experience.

—*Erma Bombeck*

$\mathcal{T}$hough motherhood is the most important of all the professions—requiring more knowledge than any other department in human affairs—there is no attention given to preparation for this office.

—*Elizabeth Cady Stanton*

$\mathcal{I}$ had already found that
motherhood was a
profession by itself, just like school
teaching and lecturing, and that once
one was launched on such a career, she
owed it to herself to become as expert as
possible in the practice of her profession.

—*Ida B. Wells*

When I broke from modeling, it felt wonderful because I stopped thinking of myself as a pretty face. If I take time off from acting for motherhood, my life will deepen in the same way. I feel as if I've got my membership now in an exclusive club and I plan on enjoying it. Acting can wait.

—*Andie MacDowell*

$\mathcal{I}$ looked on child rearing not only as a work of love and duty but as a profession that was fully as interesting and challenging as any honorable profession in the world and one that demanded the best that I could bring to it.

—*Rose Kennedy*

$\mathcal{W}$ith animals you don't see males
caring for the offspring. It's a
woman's prerogative and duty,
and a privilege.

—*Princess Grace of Monaco*

I never thought that you should be rewarded for the greatest privilege of life.

—*Mary Roper Coker*
("Mother of the Year," 1958)

$\mathcal{M}$otherhood affords an instant identity. First, through wifehood, you are somebody's wife; then you are somebody's mother. Both give not only identity, but status and stardom of a kind.

—*Betty Rollin*

$\mathcal{O}$f course, everybody knows that the greatest thing about Motherhood is the "Sacrifices," but it is quite a shock to find out that they begin so far ahead of time.

—*Anita Loos*

Over the years I have learned that motherhood is much like an austere religious order, the joining of which obligates one to relinquish all claims to personal property.

—*Nancy Stahl*

$\mathcal{M}$aternity is on the face of it an unsocial experience. The selfishness that a woman has learned to stifle or to dissemble where she alone is concerned, blooms freely and unashamed on behalf of her offspring.

—*Emily James Putnam*

he central paradox of motherhood
is that while our children become
the absolute center of our lives, they
must also push us back out in the world.
. . . But motherhood that can narrow our
lives can also broaden them. It can make
us focus intensely on the moment and
invest heavily in the future.

—*Ellen Goodman*

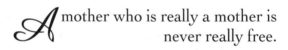

$\mathcal{A}$ mother who is really a mother is never really free.

—*Honoré de Balzac*

$\mathcal{H}$owever diligent she may be, however dedicated, no mother can escape the larger influences of culture, biology, fate . . . until we can actually live in a society where mothers and children genuinely matter, ours is an essentially powerless responsibility. Mothers carry out most of the work, but most of the rules governing our lives are shaped by outside influences.

—*Mary Kay Blakely*

$\mathcal{L}$ife is nothing but a series of
crosses for us mothers.

— *Colette*

$\mathcal{W}$hat a price we pay for the glory
of motherhood . . .

—*Isadora Duncan*

To bear and rear the majestic race to which they can never fully belong! To live vicariously forever, through their sons, the daughters being only another vicarious link! What a supreme and magnificent martyrdom!

—*Charlotte Perkins Gilman*

$\mathcal{M}$otherhood is a wonderful thing—
what a pity to waste it
on children.

—*Judith Pugh*

$\mathcal{M}$otherhood has . . . for many women ceased to be the sweet secret dream of the maiden, the glad hope of the wife, the deep regret of the aging woman who has not had this yearning satisfied.

—*Ellen Key*

When motherhood becomes the fruit of a deep yearning, not the result of ignorance or accident, its children will become the foundation of a new race.

—*Margaret Sanger*

$\mathcal{A}$waken the womanhood of
America to free the
motherhood of the world!

—*Margaret Sanger*

$\mathcal{F}$oremost among the barriers to equality is the system which ignores the mother's service to Society in making a home and rearing children. The mother is still the uncharted servant of the future, who receives from her husband, at *his* discretion, a share in *his* wages.

—*Katherine Anthony*

*C*ivilization, stretching up to recognize that every child is a portion of state wealth, may presently make some movement to recognize maternity as a business or office needing time and strength, not as a mere passing detail thrown in among mountains of other slavery.

—*Miles Franklin*

$\mathcal{M}$otherhood is sacred in America. Even New Yorkers want their mothers to have every attention.

—*Rex Yeage*

$\mathcal{T}$ake motherhood: nobody ever thought of putting it on a moral pedestal until some brash feminist pointed out, about a century ago, that the pay is lousy and the career ladder nonexistent.

—*Barbara Ehrenreich*

The job description of mother is clearly in need of revision. As it stands, the shifts are twenty-four hours, for a period of approximately 1,825 consecutive days. The benefits are sorely in need of amendment: no vacations, no sick leave, no lunch hours, no breaks. Moreover, it is the only unpaid position I know of that can result in arrest if you fail to show up for work.

—*Mary Kay Blakely*

$\mathcal{M}$otherhood—an incident, an occupation, or a career, according to the mettle of the women.

—*Mary C. Beasley*

$\mathcal{M}$otherhood has relaxed me in many ways. You learn to deal with crisis. I've become a juggler, I suppose. It's all a big circus, and nobody who knows me believes I can manage, but sometimes I do.

—*Jane Seymour*

$\mathcal{M}$otherhood has a very
humanizing effect.
Everything gets reduced to essentials.

—*Meryl Streep*

$\mathcal{M}$otherhood is not meant for the fainthearted. Used frogs, skinned knees, and the insults of teenage girls are not meant for the wimpy.

—*Danielle Steele*

The toughest part of motherhood is the inner worrying and not showing it.

—*Audrey Hepburn*

$\mathcal{S}$ometimes the laughter in mothering
is the recognition of the routines
and absurdities. Sometimes, though, it's
just pure, unthinking delight.

—*Barbara Schapiro*

$\mathcal{T}$he most consistent gift and
burden of motherhood
is advice.

—*Susan Chira*

The only thing which seems to me to be eternal and natural in motherhood is ambivalence.

—*Jane Lazarre*

$\mathcal{M}$otherhood in all its guises and
permutations is more
art than science.

—Melinda M. Marshall

$\mathcal{M}$otherhood is like Albania—you can't trust the descriptions in the books, you have to go there.

—*Marni Jackson*

I have often wished for the blessing of motherhood, for it would have given me a much needed focal point for my affections. With it, and through the varied experiences that accompany it, I could perhaps have achieved something better than that which I have attained up to now.

—*Jerry Lind*

$\mathcal{I}$ guess what I've really discovered is the humanizing effect of children in my life—stretching me, humbling me. Maybe my thighs aren't as thin as they used to be. Maybe my getaways aren't as glamorous. Still, I like the woman that motherhood has helped me to become.

—*Susan Lapinski*

Wisdom for the Modern Mother

There is only one image in this culture of the "good mother." . . . She is quietly strong, selflessly giving, undemanding, ambitious; she is receptive and intelligent in only a moderate, concrete way; she is of even temperament, almost always in control of her emotions. She loves her children completely and unambivalently. Most of us are not like her.

—*Jane Lazarre*

$\mathcal{T}$he ideal mother, like the ideal
marriage, is a fiction.

—*Milton R. Sapirstein*

$\mathcal{I}$'m not a cookie-baking mother. Well, that's not true. I am a cookie-baking mother. I'm exactly a cookie-baking mother, but I'm not a traditional cookie-baking mother.

—*Cher*

The most important thing she's learned over the years was that there was no way to be a perfect mother and a million ways to be a good one.

—*Jill Churchill*

$\mathcal{B}$ut while being a mother is admittedly a lifelong preoccupation, it cannot, should not, must not be a lifelong occupation.

—*Melinda M. Marshall*

$\mathcal{O}$ur bodies are shaped to bear children, and our lives are a working-out of the process of creation. All our ambitions and intelligence are beside that great elemental point.

—*Phyllis McGinley*

$\mathcal{I}$f women's role in life is limited
solely to housewife/mother, it
clearly ends when she can no longer
bear children and the children she has
borne leave home.

— *Betty Friedan*

*T*hough I will never be found unnatural, yet will I not, while I live, beggar myself for my cradle, if I may prevent it.

—*Elizabeth Hoby Russell*

What is sad for women of my generation is that they weren't supposed to work if they had families. What were they to do when the children were grown—watch raindrops coming down the windowpane?

—*Jacqueline Kennedy Onassis*

$\mathcal{A}$mericans have internalized the value that mothers of young children should be mothers first and foremost, and not paid workers. The result is that a substantial amount of confusion, ambivalence, guilt, and anxiety is experienced by working mothers. Our cultural expectation of mothers and the realities of female participation in the labor force are directly contradictory.

—*Ruth E. Zambrana*

For women the wage gap sets up an infuriating Catch-22 situation. They do the housework because they earn less, and they earn less because they do the housework.

—*Sylvia Ann Hewlett*

*E*very mother is a working mother.

—*Modern proverb*

$\mathcal{I}$ have a brain and a uterus,
and I use both.

—*Pat Schroeder,*
in answer to the question,
"How can you be both a lawmaker and a mother?"

$\mathcal{I}$ want to emphasize that for a queen the task of being a mother is just as important as it is for every other Netherlands woman.

—*Queen Juliana,*
in her inauguration address

You think, dear Johannes, that because I occasionally lay something aside I am giving too many concerts. But think of my responsibilities—seven children still dependent on me, five who have yet to be educated.

—*Clara Schumann,*
in a letter to Johannes Brahms

*A*ny mother could perform the
jobs of several air-traffic
controllers with ease.

—*Lisa Alther*

$\mathcal{W}$hen I had my daughter, I learned
what the sound of one hand
clapping is—it's a woman holding an
infant in one arm and a pen in the other.

—*Kate Braverman*

When her biographer says of an Italian woman poet, "during some years her Muse was intermitted," we do not wonder at the fact when he casually mentions her ten children.

—*Anna Garlin Spencer*

*R*eminds me of what one of mine wrote in a third-grade piece on how her mother spent her time. She reported "one half time on home, one half time on outside things, one half time writing."

—*Charlotte Montgomery*

$\mathcal{B}$eing asked to decide between your passion for work and your passion for children was like being asked by your doctor whether you preferred him to remove your brain or your heart.

—*Mary Kay Blakely*

$\mathcal{M}$odern women are squeezed between the devil and the deep blue sea, and there are no lifeboats out there in the form of public policies designed to help these women combine their roles as mothers and workers.

—*Sylvia Ann Hewlett*

$\mathcal{A}$t work, you think of the children you've left at home. At home, you think of the work you've left unfinished. Such a struggle is unleashed within yourself: your heart is rent.

—*Golda Meir*

You need to analyze your career, how dedicated you are to it. You've got to face the issue of how ambivalent you are about motherhood and ask yourself how much your life would be enriched by children and how much you're willing to sacrifice.

—*Marian Faux*

*I*t was almost two years ago, while awaiting the imminent birth of my second child, that I decided to start working part-time. This would have been unthinkable to me when I was younger. At twenty-five I should have worn a big red A on my chest; it would have stood for ambition so brazen and burning that it would have reduced Hester Prynne's transgression to pale pink.

—*Anna Quindlen*

$\mathcal{I}$ have often felt that I cheated my children a little. I was never so totally theirs as most mothers are. I gave to audiences what belonged to my children, got back from audiences the love that my children longed to give me.

—*Eleanor Roosevelt*

The child-rearing years are relatively short in our increased life span. It is hard for young women caught between diapers and formulas to believe, but there are years and years of freedom ahead. I regret my impatience to get on with my career. I wish I'd relaxed, allowed myself the luxury of watching the world through my little girl's eyes.

—*Eda LeShan*

You have a lifetime to work, but children are only young once.

— *Polish proverb*

Bibliography

A. K. Adams. *The Home Book of Humorous Quotations.* New York: Dodd, Mead & Co., 1969.

Robert Andrews, ed. *The Columbia Dictionary of Quotations.* New York: Columbia University Press, 1993.

Mary Biggs. *The Columbia Book of Quotations by Women.* New York: Columbia University Press, 1996.

Bruce Bohle. *The Home Book of American Quotations.* New York: Dodd, Mead & Co., 1967.

Robert and Mary Collison. *Dictionary of Foreign Quotations.* New York: Facts on File, 1980.

Henry Davidoff. *The Pocket Book of Quotations.* New York: Pocket Books, 1952.

Eugene Ehrlic and Marshall De Bruhl, eds. *The International Thesaurus of Quotations*. New York: Harper Collins, 1996.

Berger Evans. *Dictionary of Quotations*. New York: Delacorte Press, 1968.

Susan Ginsberg, ed. *Family Wisdom: The 2,000 Most Important Things Ever Said About Parenting, Children, and Family Life*. New York: Columbia University Press, 1996.

Jennifer Habel. *For Mom*. New York: Peter Pauper Press, 1995.

Alec Lewis. *The Quotable Quotations Book*. New York: Thomas Y. Crowell, 1980.

Rosalie Maggio, ed. *The New Beacon Book of Quotations by Women*. Boston: Beacon Press, 1996.

Fred Metcalf. *The Penguin Dictionary of Modern Humorous Quotations*. New York: Viking, 1986.

Margaret Miner and Hugh Rawson. *American Heritage Dictionary of American Quotations.* New York: Penguin Books, 1997.

Margaret Miner and Hugh Rawson. *The New International Dictionary of Quotations.* 2nd ed. New York: Signet, 1993.

Dierdre Mullane. *Words to Make My Dream Children Live.* New York: Doubleday, 1995.

Tillie Olsen, ed. *Mother to Daughter, Daughter to Mother, Mothers on Mothering.* Old Westbury, New York: The Feminist Press, 1984.

Elaine Partnow. *The Quotable Woman 1800–1975.* Los Angeles: Corwin Books, 1977.

Elaine Partnow. *The Quotable Woman from Eve to 1799.* New York: Facts on File, 1985.

Karen Payne, ed. *Between Ourselves: Letters Between Mothers and Daughters.* Boston: Houghton Mifflin, 1983.

Herbert V. Prochnow and Herbert V. Prochnow, Jr. *A Treasury of Humorous Quotations*. New York: Harper & Row, 1969.

William Safire and Leonard Safir. *Words of Wisdom*. New York: Simon and Schuster, 1989.

Ned Sherrin. *The Oxford Dictionary of Humorous Quotations*. Oxford: Oxford University Press, 1995.

Motherhood. Philadelphia: Running Press, 1991.

Mothers: A Tribute. Kansas City: Andrews and McMeel, 1992.

The Oxford Dictionary of Quotations. 3rd ed. Oxford: Oxford University Press, 1979.

The Quotable Woman. Philadelphia: The Running Press, 1991.